CODING
FOR
KIDS

CREATE YOUR OWN
ANIMATED STORIES
WITH SCRATCH

SCRATCH PROJECTS BY CODER KIDS

ILLUSTRATIONS BY VALENTINA FIGUS

SCRATCH 2.0

VARIABLES

STAGE **OBJECT**

MOVEMENT

SPRITE

PROJECTS

CLICK

LOOP

LEVELS

DIRECTION

RANDOM NUMBERS

FOREVER

BACKDROP ARROW **CLICK**

CONTENTS

WHY LEARN PROGRAMMING?

"Don't just buy a new video game, make one. Don't just download the latest app, help design it. Don't just play on your phone, program it."

Barack Obama

Today the concept of computational thinking plays an essential role in the new frontiers of education. The term does not refer to the ability to use a computer, but rather the ability to solve problems computationally, which is to say by breaking them up into little sub-problems to be solved in order.

It is becoming more and more widely accepted that this ability ought to be promoted alongside language and basic math skills in elementary school education.

This series is designed to introduce kids to the basic concepts of programming. Using a language created especially for them (Scratch 2.0), young readers can learn to code and create various games from the very simple to the more complex. But our goal is not train young programmers: by introducing them to programming the book seeks to teach children to express their creativity with a new tool, to find new, original and effective solutions to problems, and above all to allow them to see the beauty and the possibility of creating their own projects and realizing their own ideas from scratch, from a blank page.

Our goal is to encourage children not to experience technology passively, but to understand and see it for what it is: a very powerful tool for bringing their ideas to life.

The book is made up of 6 projects that get progressively more difficult, each of which leads to the creation of a short animated story or mini videogame. By means of intuitive tasks, each chapter will provide readers with the essential tools for programming.

We will begin with an overview that explains in detail how Scratch is used, but the book is designed so that you can also start directly from the first project. At the beginning of each chapter, readers will find an explanation of the game they will be creating, and the list of materials to use (available for download from the site indicated in the following page). Then, the procedure to follow to create the game will be illustrated step by step.

During the project, there will be some boxes, indicated by a magnifying glass, which will explain in greater detail some of several key concepts for using Scratch independently, while others feature in-depth looks at various topics.

At the end of each project readers will find a challenge, a modification to the project to make on their own; the solution to them can be found at the end of the book. We would advise that all users try to complete these, in order to test themselves and verify how well they have understood what has been taught during the project.

THE SITE

A minisite has been created to support this series, reachable at the address www.coding.whitestar.it.

Here children will find characters and backdrops with which to customize their projects. Naturally the games also work with different images, as long as they have the right format.

On our site all the materials are in SVG format, but Scratch also supports PNG, JPG, and GIF.

The materials and games contained in this book and on the site are the property of the Publisher. They may be freely used and reproduced, exclusively for non-commercial purposes.

WHAT DOES PROGRAMMING MEAN?

Programming means giving commands to a computer in a language that it can understand.

A program, therefore, transforms the computer into a tool that is useful for a certain task, by simply telling the machine how it must behave and on what occasion. The commands written by a programmer must be very precise and have to take into account every possibility, because computers don't have the ability to think autonomously.

Algorithms

An algorithm is a precise and ordered series of instructions to obtain a result. Take for example how to explain to a robot how to reach a destination in a grid such as this one.

In order to reach C3 starting from A1, the robot could take the following steps: move 1 box to the right 2 times.

Move up 1 box 2 times. This is a very simple example of an algorithm.

Obviously there's never just one possible solution to a problem!

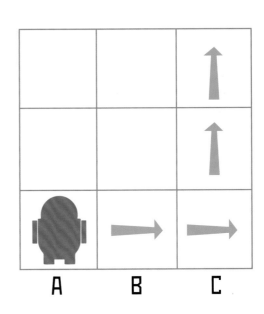

SCRATCH 2.0

"Scratch is a project of the Lifelong Kindergarten Group at the MIT Media Lab. It is provided free of charge.
Scratch helps young people learn to think creatively, reason systematically, and work collaboratively — essential skills for life in the 21st century.

With Scratch, you can program your own interactive stories, games, and animations — and share your creations with others in the online community."

[https://scratch.mit.edu/about/]

The projects in this book are designed for the version 2.0 of Scratch, but there is also an older version (1.4).
Scratch is not only a programming language: it is also a programming environment, a community, a website, and a cloud platform where users can upload their projects.
There are two ways of using Scratch: you can either use the online editor or download the program on your computer, so that you can use it even without an Internet connection.

ONLINE

To use Scratch online just go to the website scratch.mit.edu and join the Scratch community by creating an account. We suggest helping your children with this part, as personal data will be requested.
After making an account, with the username and password that you have chosen you can log in to your own personal space and start creating.
The projects created remain private, unless you yourself decide to share them.

OFFLINE

To use Scratch offline, you can download the program from the official site: click on the link scratch.mit.edu/scratch2download and follow the instructions for installing it.
There is no need to create an account to use Scratch offline.
In both versions, by clicking on [?] you will find useful suggestions that can help you begin to study, or explore further, the topics discussed in this book.

Adobe AIR

If it is not already installed on your computer, download and install the latest version of **Adobe AIR**

Editor Offline di Scratch (Beta)

Then download and install the **Scratch 2.0 Offline Editor**

Support materials

Need help getting started?
Here are some useful resources.

Starter Projects
Getting Started Guide
Scratch Cards

Sprite, Stage, Script

SPRITES

The 2D characters and objects that you will use in Scratch are called Sprites. Scratch lets you to choose them from its library, but you can also design them yourself, upload them from your computer, or create them from photos.

x: 240 y: 30

Sprites   New sprite:

STAGE

The stage in Scratch manages all the backdrops of your projects.
Like with the Sprites, you can select backdrops from the library, design them, upload them from your computer, or use a photo.

New background:

Upload a Sprite from the Scratch library

Upload a backdrop from the Scratch library

Design your Sprite or your backdrop

Upload your Sprite or your backdrop from the computer

Take a photo from the Webcam to create your Sprite or backdrop

SCRIPTS

Scripts are the instructions and the commands that you give to the Sprites or to the Stage.

SEQUENTIALITY

The computer carries out the commands from top to bottom, one at a time.

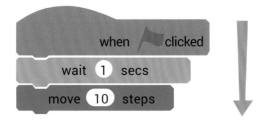

ACTIVE SCRIPT

When Scratch is performing a script, this lights up!

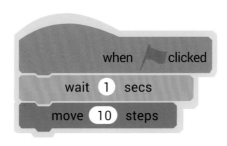

Areas

Scratch 2.0 is divided into 5 main areas. Let's go through them together.

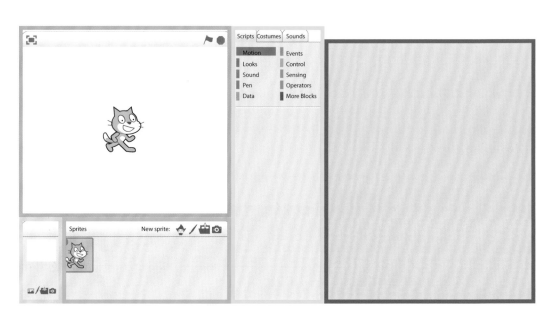

Game screen: here is where your stories and games come to life. From this area you can press:

Start the game.

Stop the game.

Activate game mode. Careful! In game mode you can only play, not make changes! To return and make adjustments to the project click on the same key again.

Stage Area: this contains the backdrops of your project

Sprite Area: this contains your characters and objects

Blocks Area: this contains all the commands for Scratch

Scripts Area: is designed to allow you to give commands to each of your backdrops and objects

Tools

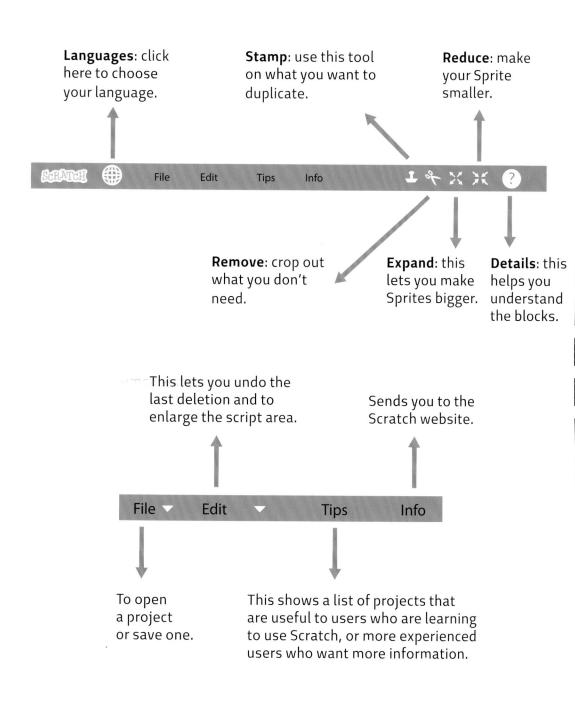

Languages: click here to choose your language.

Stamp: use this tool on what you want to duplicate.

Reduce: make your Sprite smaller.

Remove: crop out what you don't need.

Expand: this lets you make Sprites bigger.

Details: this helps you understand the blocks.

This lets you undo the last deletion and to enlarge the script area.

Sends you to the Scratch website.

To open a project or save one.

This shows a list of projects that are useful to users who are learning to use Scratch, or more experienced users who want more information.

BLOCKS

Hat Blocks: hat blocks are always placed at the start of a script, and indicate where it starts. Nothing can be placed above them.

Stack Blocks: these are the blocks that you'll use the most, because they tell the components of the game WHAT they have to do. You can place other blocks above and below them.

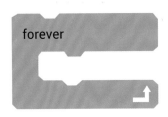

C Blocks: these tell the game IF and HOW MANY TIMES to do something. They come in a C-shape because they can wrap themselves around other blocks.

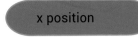

Cap Blocks: these are placed at the end of a script, and indicate the END. You cannot place any other blocks below them.

Boolean Blocks: standing out due to their hexagonal shapes, these can take on only values: TRUE or FALSE.

Reporter Blocks: these have rounded edges and can be different types of values, for examples numbers or words.

Look closely! In some of these blocks you'll find a little black triangle. If you click on it you'll open what in the computer world is known as a drop-down menu: from you can choose a different value from the one written in the block.

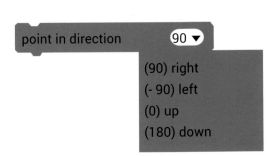

(90) right
(- 90) left
(0) up
(180) down

The blocks in Scratch are of different colors according to the category to which they belong. For example: all the commands that make the characters of your projects move are found in the motion category and are blue. In order to see a category's blocks just click on its name.

Motion	Events
Looks	Control
Sound	Sensing
Pen	Operators
Data	More Blocks

The blocks can also be joined to one another, if their form fits in the space you want to place them in.

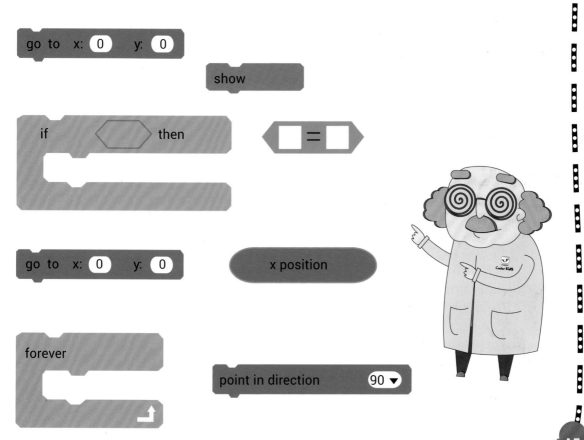

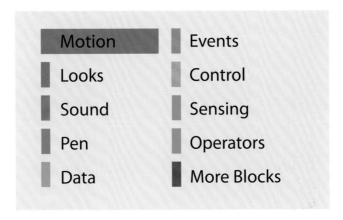

Motion: these contain the instructions that control your sprites' movement.

Looks: here you'll find the blocks that modify the appearance of everything on the scene.

Sound: want to add a bit of music to your project? You'll find what you need here.

Pen: Whether it's just to draw simple a line or to create complex visual effects, you're going to need a pen!

Data: if you click on this category you can create variables or lists. What are they? You'll find out further on!

Event: these include all the blocks that represent events or situations.

Control: the blocks in this extremely important category explain to the program how and when to activate the various scripts.

Sensing: if two objects are touching or if a key is being pressed, the sensing blocks always notice!

Operators: sometimes you need to do some math... Operators can make calculations or compare two numbers.

More blocks: this category is empty, but it lets you make your own blocks!

PANES

SPRITE PANES

Each Sprite has 3 panes:
If you select the first, Script, it will open the list of the blocks, and, to the right, the area to construct the Scripts.

The second, Costumes, contains all of the costumes of the Sprite selected, in other words all the ways that Sprite can appear.
To the right you'll see Scratch's Paint Editor, which allows you to edit the appearance of the Sprites.

The Sounds pane lets you add a sound from your Scratch library but also to record one or upload one from your computer!

STAGE PANES

The Stage also has 3 panes:
Scripts and Sounds work just like they do with Sprites.
But the second, Backdrops, is different.

Just as Sprites appears differently according to the costume they are wearing at the moment, so too the appearance of the Stage changes according to the backdrop.
If you open the Backdrops pane you'll find all of the ones you have inserted in your project. Of course, you can also add more of them!

PROJECTS

Here's where your adventure into the world
of programming videogames begins.

If you don't have Scratch 2.0 on your computer,
now's the time! Ask for help from an adult
if you need to!

Some of these games might seem easy. . . to play!
The real challenge is programming them,
from the ground up.

1.

LEVEL

THE DAWN OF A NEW DAY

1.

The Dawn of a New Day

The sun rises on your first project!

Bring to life a magical African dawn!

LEVEL:

The Game

Make the darkness disappear gradually, while the sun rises in the sky.

What You'll Learn:

- To set up a new project

- To create a simple animation

- To create effects with graphics

MATERIALS

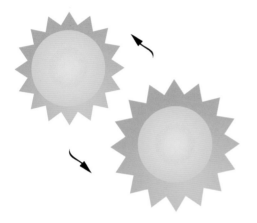

BACKDROPS

I'll explain everything! Let's take it a step at a time!

MATERIALS

On the site indicated in the introduction we've prepared everything that you'll need to create our games. You'll find various versions of each Sprite and many backdrops upon which to set their adventures.

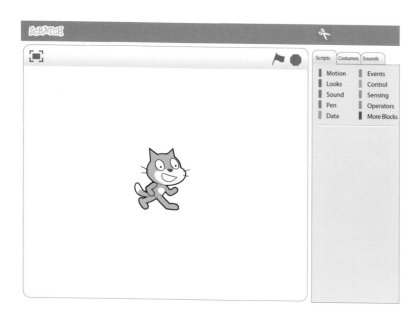

Before getting to work on our project, we have to prepare Scratch: so let's open it!

Every time you begin a new project, at the center of the screen you'll find an orange cat, the Sprite that is the symbol of Scratch.

But this time the Scratch cat won't be a character in your game, so you'll have to delete it by using the tool REMOVE.

The first step to bringing our world to life is to populate it with Sprites. But... what's a Sprite?

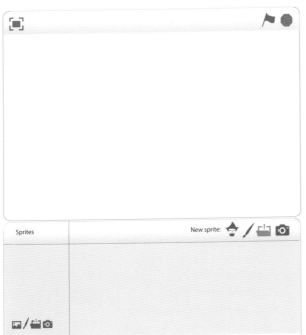

The word *sprite* refers to a mythological creature similar to a fairy or a ghost.

The characters designed in 2D like the ones we use in Scratch are known as sprites for the way they glide over fixed image, the backdrop, without being part of it.

This way of drawing and animating characters was invented in the 1970s, and made it possible to put more numerous and detailed characters into videogames. Before this innovation, the computer had to redraw the character anew every time it moved.

NOW WE CAN CHOOSE OUR SPRITE!

In the section New Sprite, click on the folder icon to upload a sprite from your computer, after downloading it from the site.

To learn how to download the Sprite from the site, go back to Chapter 1 of this book.

CHOOSE THE SPRITE OF THE NIGHT AND OF THE SUN

Careful! It's important to insert the Sprites in a precise order: imagine that Sprites are sheets of paper placed one on top of another. At the top of the pile there will be the sun, under it the night, and under the night the backdrop of the day.

The backdrop
is a fixed image,
which the characters
of our stories
move on.

Like with Sprites,
you can choose to draw
your own backdrops,
get them from
somewhere else,
upload them from the
Scratch library, or add
them directly from your
computer's camera.

Click on the folder icon, in the section New Backdrop, to upload
a backdrop from your computer. Again, remember to download
it first from the site.

WHY HAVE WE USED A BACKDROP FOR THE DAYTIME SKY AND A SPRITE FOR NIGHTTIME SKY?

Simple!

In order to create the effect we want, we have to put the night in the front, to then make it slowly dissolve leaving the sun of the day. Since we cannot overlap two backdrops, one of the two will have to be a sprite.

ATTENTION!

A **Backdrop** is not the same thing as the **Stage**.

The stage is an element of Scratch you can give instructions to. With the stage you can change the backdrop and manage other aspects that don't concern a single Sprite but the game in general.

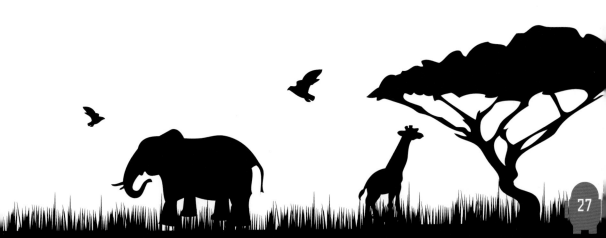

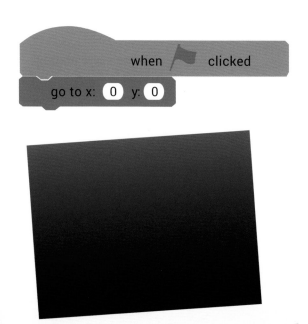

Every Sprite always has to know what to do and when to do it, and you'll be the one to tell it!
To begin, let's move over to the Script section.

For more info about the Scratch Areas, go to page 12.

Drag the first block into the work area:
WHEN GREEN FLAG CLICKED.
The green flag is what sets off what we have programmed, whether it's a game or just an animation.

Under this command, all the instructions must be place which the Sprite will have to carry when the program starts.

Under this, place the block GO TO X: 0, Y: 0.
This way, as soon as the green flag is clicked, the character will be positioned at the center of the Stage.

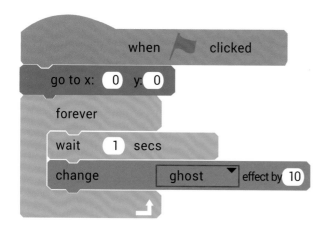

when ⚑ clicked

go to x: 0 y: 0

forever

wait 1 secs

change ghost ▾ effect by 10

To make our Sprite dissolve, we will use one of Scratch's graphic effects: the GHOST EFFECT.

Take a FOREVER block and put it under the last block you positioned.

Inside the FOREVER block, place the block CHANGE GHOST EFFECT BY 10. Add the command WAIT 1 SECS, so that the Sprite disappears more slowly.

FOREVER

Blocks like FOREVER are known as loops. Instructions of this kind are used in programming to make a series of commands repeat. In Scratch, a FOREVER repeats the instructions it contains to infinity, in the order they're arranged in. Well... not quite forever, more like until the program is closed.

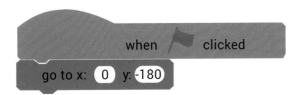

Like we did with the Sprite of the night sky, let's give a starting position to the Sprite.

This time, when the green flag is clicked, we need the sun to be low, at the center. To do this, take the block GO TO X: 0, Y: -180 and place it under the block WHEN GREEN FLAG CLICKED.

. . .RISES. . .

From the bottom, the sun will have to rise to the top of the stage, or of the sky!

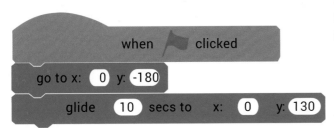

Take the block GLIDE 10 SECS TO and set the point of arrival to X: 0, Y: 130. This position will make the sun come up in the upper center of the Stage.

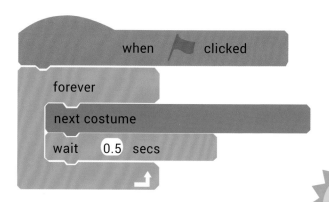

when 🚩 clicked

forever

next costume

wait 0.5 secs

To create the effect of the sun shining, we'll make the Sprite change its costume continuously, thus creating our first animation!

Take a FOREVER loop and make sure that the sun continues to repeat the two commands NEXT COSTUME and WAIT 0.5 SECS.

COSTUMES

Sprites' costumes are the way they appear on screen. But even if its appearance changes, a Sprite remains itself. Just like you are still yourself even if you change your clothes! The costumes are all the ways that our Sprites can appear in the game. The cool thing is that, working on a computer, there are no limits to our imagination: a dinosaur can easily turn into an apple at our command. If you want to take advantage of all the potential Scratch offers, you must absolutely learn how to use this tool!

ANIMATIONS:

An animation is the illusion, created with various techniques, that an object on the screen is really moving.

The method that we'll be using is the one used in cartoons that aren't three-dimensional. It consists in putting together a number of images, each one slightly different than the one before, and making them move quickly before the viewer's eyes.

To make things easier you'll find the complete SCRIPT for both the game's Sprites below.

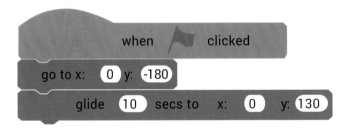

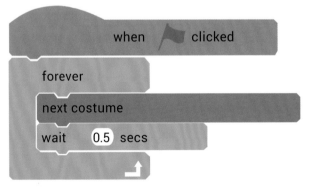

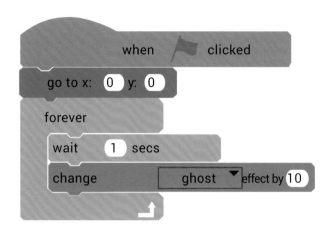

SCRIPT

In everyday English, the word "script" refers to what actors read from to learn their lines. In a program, a script is a sequence of instructions used to make it perform tasks. Imagine that all the characters that you insert into Scratch are actors in your game, each with their part to play.

Every script, for example the one in image above, begins with an Event, like WHEN GREEN FLAG CLICKED, and stops with the last instruction given, or when the red light is clicked.

2.

LEVEL

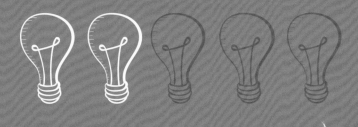

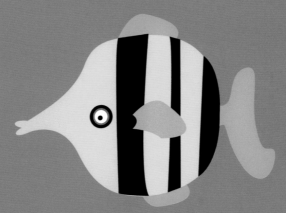

"JUST KEEP SWIMMING!"

2.

"Just Keep Swimming!"

**Bring to life
your aquarium
full of colorful
fish.**

Level:

The Game

Let your fish
swim freely among
the bubbles!

You can choose from
among many types
of fish to customize
your aquarium!

What You'll Learn:

- To clone Sprites

- To use randomness

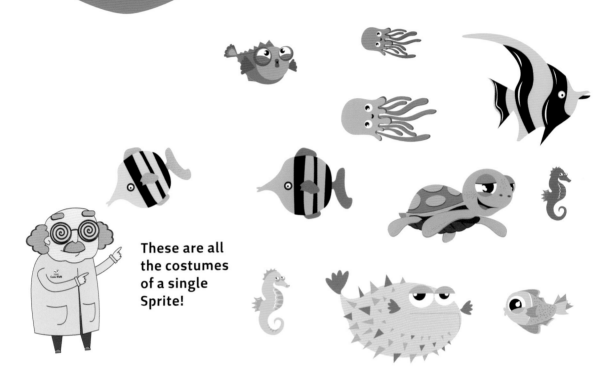

These are all the costumes of a single Sprite!

BACKDROPS

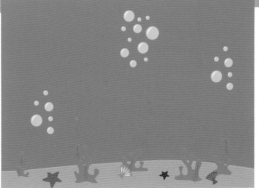

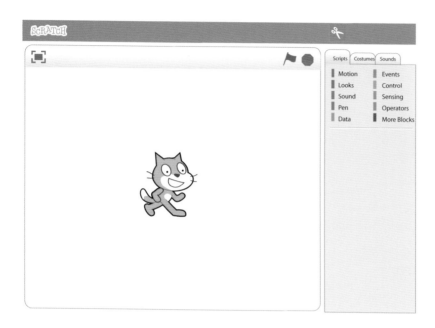

Let's prepare Scratch to work on a new project.

Open Scratch, delete the cat, and give a name to the new project by clicking on FILE > SAVE AS. Then choose the Sprites and the backdrops you need for the new game.

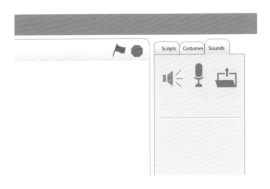

Who says it's quiet inside of an aquarium?

Add the sound of bubbles gurgling to the animation, to create the right atmosphere.

Select the Sound pane and click on the symbol highlighted to choose a sound from the Scratch library.

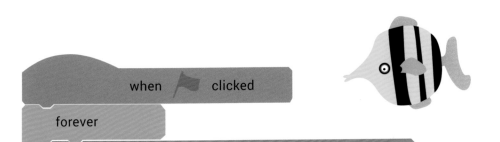

Now take the block PLAY SOUND BUBBLES UNTIL DONE and put it in a FOREVER loop. Make everything start when the green flag is clicked. This way the program will reproduce the sound from the beginning of the game, and every time the sound ends, it will restart it.

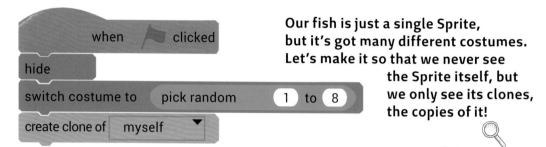

Our fish is just a single Sprite, but it's got many different costumes. Let's make it so that we never see the Sprite itself, but we only see its clones, the copies of it!

Make the Sprite hide at the beginning of the animation, and then make it choose randomly from among its costumes by inserting the Operator PICK RANDOM NUMBER in the block SWITCH COSTUME TO.

Then take the block CREATE CLONE OF MYSELF.
If you try to click on the green flag nothing will happen yet: for now we've only created a single clone of the fish, and it hasn't shown itself yet!

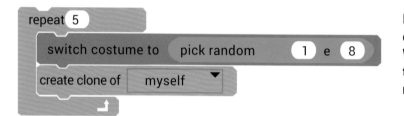

How many fish do you want? We can clone the Sprite multiple times!

Make the blocks SWITCH COSTUME TO and CREATE CLONE OF MYSELF repeat by putting them a loop of REPEAT 5.
The program will then carry out the loop five times, creating five fish: first choose randomly from among the Sprite's costumes. Then generate a clone with the chosen costume and start over from the beginning.

CLONES

Scratch gives us the possibility to clone Sprites, that is, to duplicate them. There are 3 blocks we need when we work with clones:
1. CREATE CLONE OF. . . : create a clone of the Sprite chosen.
2. WHEN I START AS A CLONE: this is a starting event. Under this block put everything that the clone has to do when it is created.
3. DELETE THIS CLONE: it's important to delete clones when they are no longer needed; Scratch can manage a maximum of around 300 clones: once this number is exceeded, it stops producing them to avoid making the program too heavy.

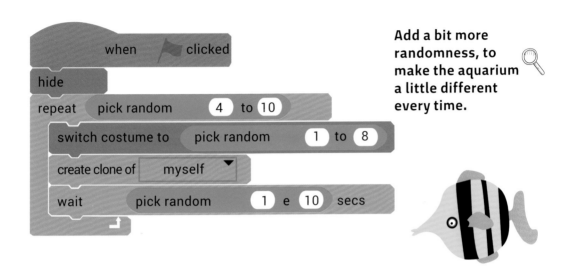

Add a bit more randomness, to make the aquarium a little different every time.

Take a PICK RANDOM NUMBER operator and put it in the place of the 5 in the loop REPEAT 5. This way the number of fish in your aquarium will always be different!

After the command CREAT CLONE OF MYSELF add the block WAIT. . . SECS, so the fish are created a few seconds after one another.

In place of the number of seconds add another PICK RANDOM NUMBER block to make this interval random too.

RANDOMNESS

Say the first number that comes to your mind. Any number, randomly!
Easy, right? Well for a computer this is so difficult as to be practically impossible. Because machines only do what they've been ordered to do. Saying "pick a random number" is, practically speaking, like saying "you decide," and a computer can't make decisions! So how is it that many of the games we have created in this book use the block "random number?"

Even though the block is called "random number," the number that is chosen is not completely random. It's actually the result of very complex operations that aim to simulate randomness as much as possible.

Now's the time to make the cloned fish appear!

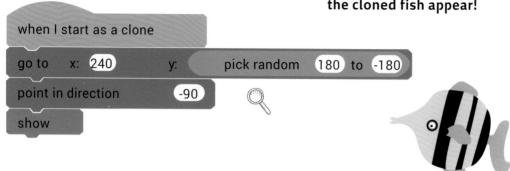

when I start as a clone

go to   x: 240   y: (pick random 180 to -180)

point in direction   -90

show

Take a block of WHEN I START AS A CLONE. Under this starting event we will define, in order, everything the clone will have to do once it has appeared.

The first thing it will have to do is to position itself at the right of the Stage, where X is 240, at a random point between the upper part (Y: 180) and the lower part (Y: -180). Immediately afterwards, it will have to turn to the left (-90) and show itself.

DIRECTION

The block POINT IN DIRECTION. . . makes the Sprite turn in the direction chosen. By clicking on the black triangle in the block you can select a direction: up (0), down (180), right (90) and left (-90), or type in a number. To make the Sprite face to the right you'll need to choose a number from 1 to 179 as indicated by the red arrow. On the other hand, if you want a Sprite to turn to the left, you'll have to use a negative number (i.e. with the − sign in front of it) from -179 to -1, as the blue arrow indicates.

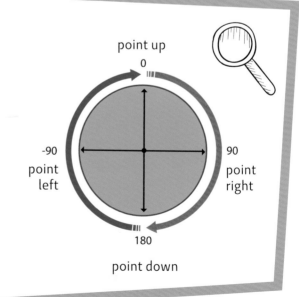

point up
0

-90
point
left

90
point
right

180

point down

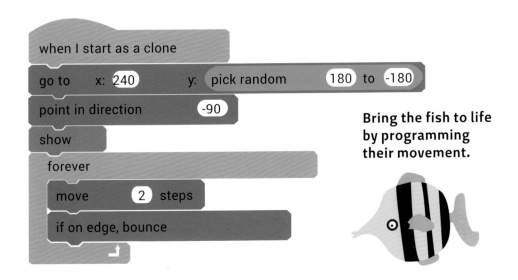

```
when I start as a clone
go to    x: 240    y:    pick random    180  to  -180
point in direction        -90
show
  forever
    move        2  steps
    if on edge, bounce
```

Bring the fish to life by programming their movement.

Take a FOREVER loop and add the blocks MOVE 2 STEPS and IF ON EDGE, BOUNCE.
This way the clone will move until it touches the edge, and then turn around and move in the opposite direction.

TRY IT!

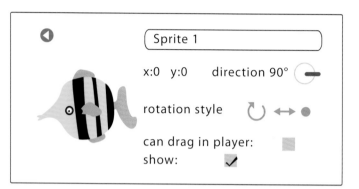

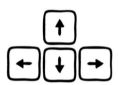

If you now try to make the fish swim, you'll notice they turn upside down: we have to solve this problem!

To make sure the Sprite doesn't flip over, change its rotation style!

Click on the  and choose the style

Scratch allows you to give Sprites three rotation styles:

Free: the Sprite rolls freely in all directions.

Right-Left: the object turns only to the right and to the left.

Blocked: the object cannot rotate.

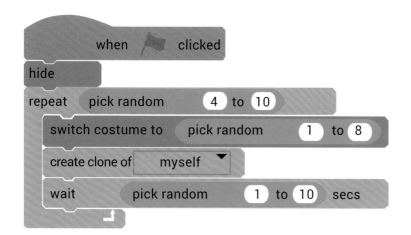

```
when [flag] clicked
hide
repeat (pick random 4 to 10)
    switch costume to (pick random 1 to 8)
    create clone of [myself ▼]
    wait (pick random 1 to 10) secs
```

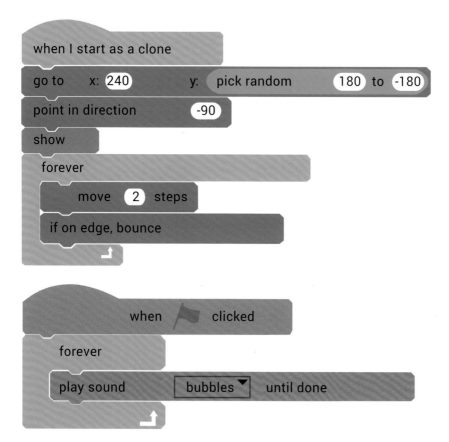

```
when I start as a clone
go to x: 240 y: (pick random 180 to -180)
point in direction -90
show
forever
    move 2 steps
    if on edge, bounce
```

```
when [flag] clicked
forever
    play sound [bubbles ▼] until done
```

45

CHALLENGE

BUBBLES

Make the scene more dynamic!

Give a nice touch to the aquarium
by adding bubbles that start at the
bottom and rise to center of the Stage.

A hint:

Use clones!

3.

LEVEL

THE MATH DRAGON

3.

THE MATH DRAGON

A dragon with a mad passion for numbers is blocking the road to the castle. It will let us pass only if we answer 3 math questions correctly!

LEVEL:

THE GAME

In order to answer the dragon's questions, type in the answer and press the ENTER key.

????

- To program a game based on questions and answers

- To use variables

SPRITES

MATERIALS

BACKDROPS

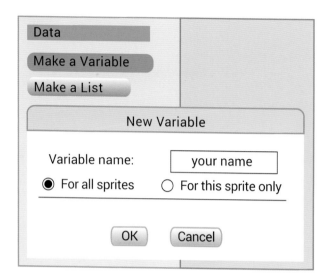

Let's make it so that the dragon knows the name of who's playing!

In the category DATA, click on CREATE A VARIABLE.

Now give it a name: since it will be representing the name of our player, we'll call it "your name."

Your name is of interest to the Sprite of the dragon, not to the whole game: so set the variable FOR THIS SPRITE ONLY.
As soon as you click on OK, new command blocks will be created.
Let's go through them together!

A variable is information that has been given a name, and which the computer has been ordered to memorize. Here's a simple example:

WHAT IS YOUR AGE?

Naturally, you won't have any difficulty answering this question. This is because ever since you were little you have memorized a piece of information (a variable), called "my age," which represents in numerical form the years that have passed since you were born.

A variable, as the name suggests, can vary: your age changes every time it's your birthday, but it's always "your age."

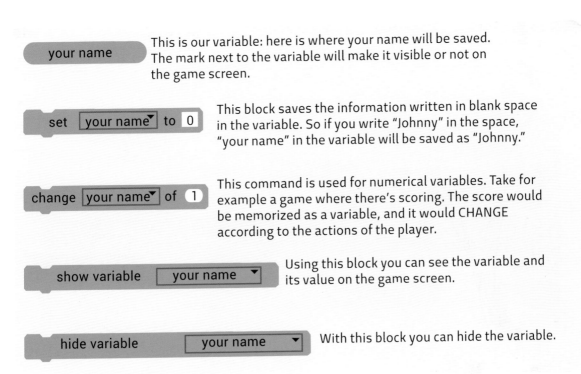

your name

This is our variable: here is where your name will be saved. The mark next to the variable will make it visible or not on the game screen.

set your name▾ to 0

This block saves the information written in blank space in the variable. So if you write "Johnny" in the space, "your name" in the variable will be saved as "Johnny."

change your name▾ of 1

This command is used for numerical variables. Take for example a game where there's scoring. The score would be memorized as a variable, and it would CHANGE according to the actions of the player.

show variable   your name ▾

Using this block you can see the variable and its value on the game screen.

hide variable   your name ▾

With this block you can hide the variable.

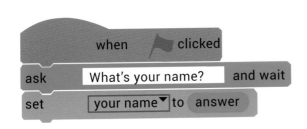

Take an ASK block from the sensing category.

This block makes the question that is written in the blank space appear in a word bubble of the Sprite, then it pauses the script until the player types an answer and presses Enter. Save the answer in the block ANSWER.

Now take the block SET "YOUR NAME" TO and place the block ANSWER in its blank space. This way the answer just given will be saved in the variable "your name," and the dragon will remember it for the whole game!

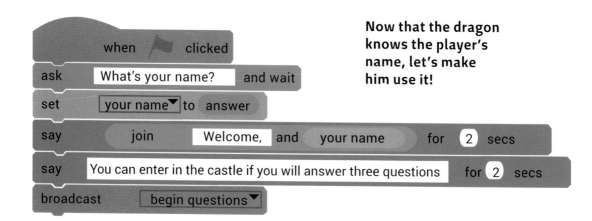

Now that the dragon knows the player's name, let's make him use it!

```
when 🚩 clicked
ask  What's your name?  and wait
set  your name ▼ to  answer
say  join  Welcome,  and  your name  for 2 secs
say  You can enter in the castle if you will answer three questions  for 2 secs
broadcast  begin questions ▼
```

Add, under SET "YOUR NAME" TO, two blocks of SAY. . . FOR 2 SECS.

In the blank space of the first one, put a JOIN Operator.

This way there will be space in the block for the word "Welcome," but also for the variable "your name."

Since in the last block you saved your name inside the variable, now the dragon will greet you with your name!

In the second SAY block write the rules for the game. Then, tell the entire game that the questions are about to start, by sending the message "begin questions."

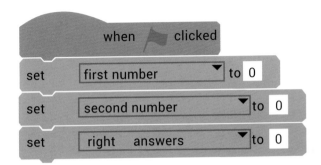

set first number to 0

set second number to 0

set right answers to 0

In a moment the dragon will start asking you questions. In this case, they will be about multiplication tables.

Since multiplication tables are operations made up of two numbers, and the two numbers always have to be different from one question to the next, you need to create two more variables: "first number" and "second number."

Also these variables are only of interest to the dragon Sprite, so set them "For this Sprite only."

The game will also have to count the number of correct answers the player gives. So we'll need another variable. But this time the entire program has to know it, so set it "For all Sprites."

Now make it so that, at the beginning of the game, the variables are equal to 0.

It the programming world this operation is called INITIALIZATION.

INITIALIZATION

The variables need to reset themselves to zero every time the green flag is clicked. Otherwise, a player who begins a new game will find the score of the previous game! It's important that the programmer remembers to initialize all the variables, which means explaining to the game what value they must have at the beginning of the game.

MULTIPLICATION TABLES

Let's make it so that the two numbers the dragon asks us to multiply are always different!

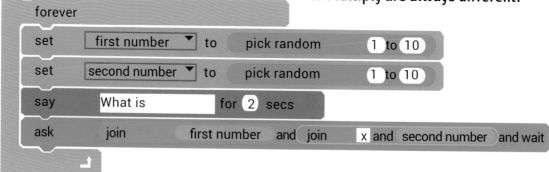

Place this Script under the dragon's last SAY block. Careful: you need to join two JOIN operators in order to have enough spaces.

The dragon, FOREVER, will do these things in order:

1. He'll pick the first number to multiply, randomly between 1 and 10.
2. He'll pick the second number, again at random between 1 and 10.
3. He'll say "What is..." for 2 seconds.
4. He'll ask for the sum of the multiplication of the two random numbers, and wait for an answer.

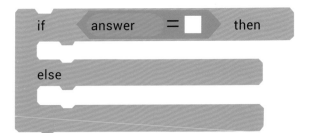

The dragon knows the answer. He'll notice whether the answer is right or wrong!

Place this script under the last block ASK... and WAIT that you inserted.

As we've already seen, the ASK block waits until the enter key has been pressed, then it saves, in the ANSWER block, the answer the player has typed in.

Now the dragon will need to check whether the answer is correct or not. How? Simple! Take the command IF... THEN... ELSE and in the space next to the IF put an [... = ...] operator. Then place the block ANSWER to the left of the equal sign.

IF... THEN
The concept of IF... THEN is one of the most important in Scratch, and in programming in general. Consider the phrase: if it's sunny, I'll go to the beach.
The words "if" and "then" connect two events, so that if the CONDITION (it's sunny) is true, then by necessity the second, the CONSEQUENCE (I'll go to the beach), will also take place.
In Scratch the condition needs to be inserted in the empty hexagonal space of the block, while the consequence is placed in the internal part of the block.
IF... THEN is useful when we need to know what to do when the condition is true.

IF... THEN... ELSE
But what if it's not sunny? Then I might, for example, stay home.
IF... THEN... ELSE acts exactly like IF... THEN, except that it also lets us specify what we will do in the event the condition is false.

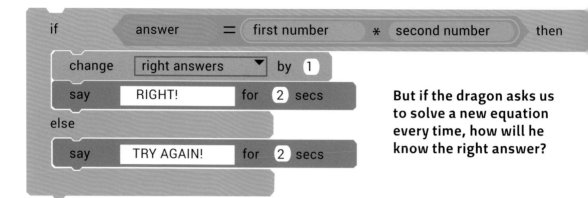

if | answer | = | first number | ✳ | second number | then

change | right answers ▼ | by 1

say | RIGHT! | for 2 secs

else

say | TRY AGAIN! | for 2 secs

But if the dragon asks us to solve a new equation every time, how will he know the right answer?

Take the math operator [... * ...] and place it to the right of the equal sign. This block carries out a multiplication between two numbers, just like a calculator.

Therefore, IF the answer is EQUAL to the "first number" multiplied by the "second number," THEN it will be correct. Or ELSE it will be wrong.

Now make it so that the dragon says a different phrase according to whether the answer is right or wrong.

Don't forget that, when you answer correctly, the answer variable has to increase by one point. Use the block CHANGE RIGHT ANSWER BY 1.

MATH OPERATORS:

The computer does very complex calculations extremely quickly: it's a real-life math dragon! In the programs you make you can therefore easily insert calculations that use the four basic operations.

Four blocks of the operator category are called "math operators."

+ Addition	* Multiplication
− Subtraction	/ Division

These blocks carry out additions, subtractions, multiplications, and divisions, and they give us the answer in the blink of an eye. Try it! Assign the command here below to a Sprite.
You'll see that the character won't say "2 + 2" but directly "4"!

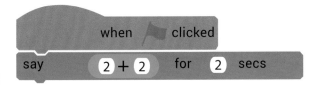

COMPARATIVE OPERATORS:

These are in the operator category, and are called "comparatives" because they compare two values. We use them to check whether a number is greater than, less than, or equal to another.

= equal to	> greater than
	< less than

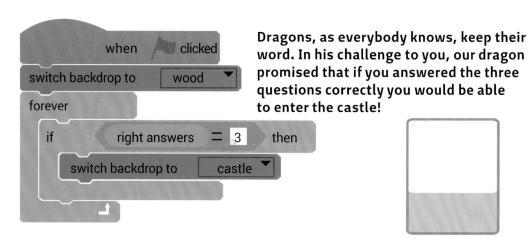

Dragons, as everybody knows, keep their word. In his challenge to you, our dragon promised that if you answered the three questions correctly you would be able to enter the castle!

```
when [flag] clicked
switch backdrop to [ wood ▼ ]
forever
    if < right answers = 3 > then
        switch backdrop to [ castle ▼ ]
```

Give the following commands to the Stage, because it's the stage that will have to change the backdrop at the right moment.

At the start of the game the backdrop will be a forest. But when the player has given the three correct answers, it will change to show that we've arrived at the castle.

In a FOREVER loop, check with an IF. . . THEN that three correct answers have been given. In that case, make the backdrop change.

```
when backdrop switches to [ castle ▼ ]
say [ Welcome ! ] for (2) secs
```

As we were saying, a dragon always keeps his promises!

When the castle backdrop appears, that dragon will welcome us.

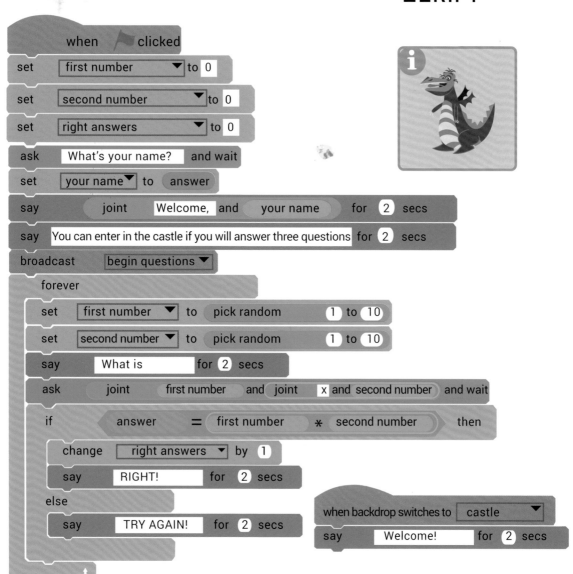

```
when [flag] clicked
set first number to 0
set second number to 0
set right answers to 0
ask What's your name? and wait
set your name to answer
say joint Welcome, and your name for 2 secs
say You can enter in the castle if you will answer three questions for 2 secs
broadcast begin questions
forever
    set first number to pick random 1 to 10
    set second number to pick random 1 to 10
    say What is for 2 secs
    ask join first number and joint x and second number and wait
    if answer = first number * second number then
        change right answers by 1
        say RIGHT! for 2 secs
    else
        say TRY AGAIN! for 2 secs
```

```
when backdrop switches to castle
say Welcome! for 2 secs
```

```
when [flag] clicked
switch backdrop to wood
forever
    if right answers = 3 then
        switch backdrop to castle
```

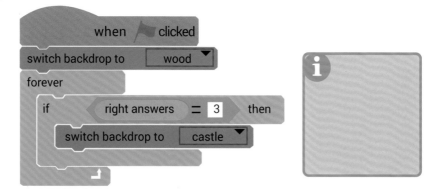

CHALLENGE

WHAT WAS THE RIGHT ANSWER?

Now, if the player gives a wrong answer, the dragon responds "try again" without giving the correct answer.

Try to make it so that the dragon also says what the correct answer was.

A hint:

Use the math operators!

4.

LEVEL

FIND
THE KEY

4.

FIND THE KEY

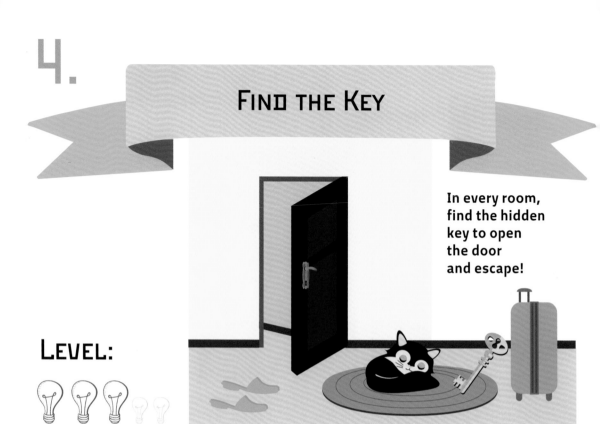

In every room, find the hidden key to open the door and escape!

LEVEL:

THE GAME

There are many ways of interacting with the Sprites on screen: click on the rug to make it move, or clap your hands to wake up the sleeping cat!

Once you've found the key, drag it over to the door with the mouse to leave the room.

WHAT YOU'LL LEARN:

- To use messages

- To create a game with levels

- New ways of interacting with Sprites: clicking, using the microphone, "drag and drop."

SPRITES

MATERIALS

BACKDROPS

YOU WIN!

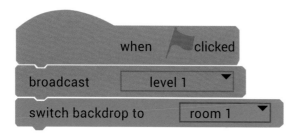

```
when  🚩 clicked
broadcast   level 1  ▼
switch backdrop to   room 1  ▼
```

At the beginning, all the actors in our game will have to know that the first level has started.

This way they'll be able to position themselves in the right spot (if they're part of the first level), or hide (if they're part of the second).

But how can we inform everyone, at the exact same time, that the first level has begun?

Simple: we'll send a MESSAGE! In the event category you'll find the block BROADCAST new message. Name the new message something that makes sense with what we have to communicate, like "Level 1."

After sending the message, the Stage will have to SWITCH BACKDROP TO ROOM 1.

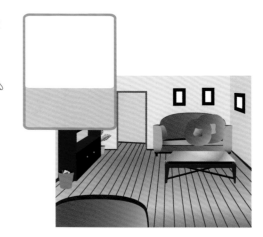

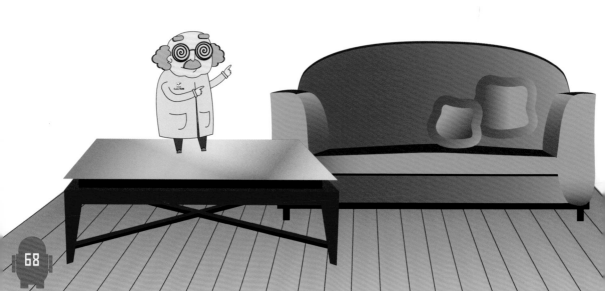

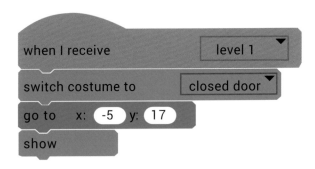

At the start of the first level the door must be closed!

When the door Sprite RECEIVES the message LEVEL 1, it will need to immediately SWITCH COSTUME TO CLOSED DOOR.

Then it will need to position itself, with the block GO TO X:, Y: at the point where you have decided to put it for this level, and then it will have to SHOW itself.

MESSAGES

The Stage and the Sprites can communicate with each other using messages.

A message is sent by an actor with the block BROADCAST, and it can be used as a condition to start another Script with the block WHEN I RECEIVE. You'll find all of these blocks in the Events category.

To send a message, just open the drop-down menu of the block BROADCAST and choose the option NEW MESSAGE. At this point you can send it, after giving it a name: ideally you would give it a name that is in line with what the message is communicating. But don't worry too much about this name: the player will never see it, as it's only used by you and the program to manage an event inside the game.

FIRST LEVEL: THE RUG

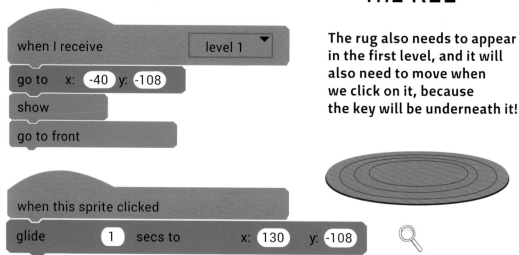

The rug also needs to appear in the first level, and it will also need to move when we click on it, because the key will be underneath it!

Place the rug where you want in the room, and then take a block of GO TO X:, Y: and put it under the event WHEN I RECEIVE LEVEL 1. The X and Y coordinates will already be the correct ones, and the rug will just have to SHOW itself.

Remember that this Sprite will be hiding the key, and so it will have to be placed above it.
Remember how? As we explained on page 25, Sprites are like pieces of paper placed one on top of another, or all on the same plane. Thus to make it so that the rug covers the key, we have to tell the rug to GO TO FRONT, so that the key will never be the one on the top of the rug.

Finally, when the player clicks on the rug, it has to glide to the left and reveal the key. Move the Sprite to the place it has to reach when it glides and then place the block GLIDE. The X and Y coordinates will again be the correct ones.

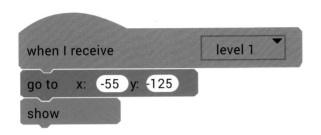

when I receive   level 1 ▼

go to   x: -55 y: -125

show

The key in the first level will also have its position and will have to appear.

Yes, the key will need to show itself, even though nobody will see as long as it is under the rug!

Choose a position in the area of the rug, fix it with the block GO To X:, Y: and then make the Sprite appear with the block SHOW.

COORDINATES

Every point of the Stage is identified by two numbers, the "coordinates," called X and Y. The X indicates the position on a horizontal line, the Y on a vertical line. The two lines intersect at the center of the screen in the point called X:0, Y:0.

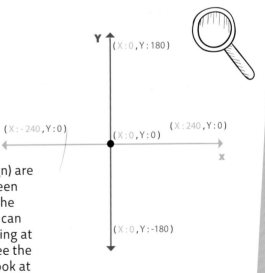

(X:0,Y:180)

(X:-240,Y:0)   (X:240,Y:0)

(X:0,Y:0)

(X:0,Y:-180)

Negative coordinates (with the minus sign) are always found in the lower part of the screen or on the left, while positive ones are in the upper part or on the right. In Scratch you can see the coordinates of the cursor by looking at the bottom right of the Stage, while to see the current coordinates of a Sprite you can look at the top right of the screen.

Every time you position a Sprite, in the Movement blocks area, the coordinates will change automatically in the blocks GO TO X:, Y: and GLIDE.

TAKE THE KEY

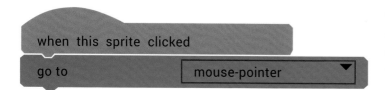

when this sprite clicked

go to (mouse-pointer ▼)

The key must be taken, dragged to the door and left there.

Up to this point you have always moved Sprites from one point to another on the Stage with the mouse, but if you try to set Scratch to game mode, you won't be able to do it anymore. Unless of course, you program the Sprite to be dragged with the mouse!

Do you remember what the game mode is? If not, go back to page 12 of the introduction.

WHEN THIS SPRITE CLICKED, it has to follow the cursor of the mouse. To achieve this, use the block GO TO MOUSE POINTER.

IF YOU TRY TO PUT SCRATCH INTO GAME MODE AND DRAG THE KEY, YOU'LL SEE THAT IT STILL DOESN'T WORK LIKE IT SHOULD! LET ME EXPLAIN!

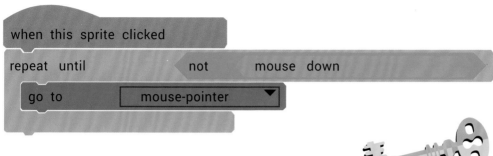

```
when this sprite clicked
repeat until        not        mouse down
    go to           mouse-pointer ▼
```

Attention!
The key has to follow the cursor of the mouse as long as the mouse button is pressed.

So once the mouse button has been released, the key must stop following the cursor.
To program this, take the loop REPEAT UNTIL and put it in the space for the condition of a NOT Operator with the sensing block MOUSE DOWN.

If you read the Script like this, it will be clearer:
From WHEN THIS SPRITE IS CLICKED, GO TO THE MOUSE POINTER UNTIL the BUTTON OF THE MOUSE is no longer held DOWN.

DRAG AND DROP

Often in games and applications, you need to drag something with the mouse or with your finger to put it down in another place.
This function is called "Drag and Drop."
Actually, as you're discovering as you program it, a Drag and Drop is made up of 3 moments:
1. The item has to be clicked.
2. It has to follow the mouse has long as it's pressed down.
3. It has to stop following it when the button is released.

Scratch contains the option "Draggable in the player," in the information for every Sprite. By activating this option, Sprites become draggable in the game mode. But this function isn't always enough to make the Drag and Drop work how it should!

OPENING THE DOOR

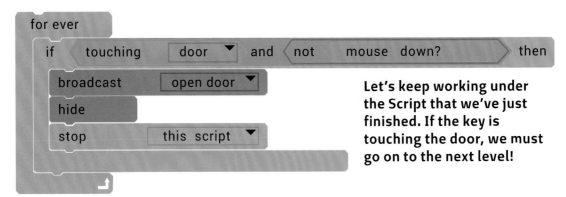

Let's keep working under the Script that we've just finished. If the key is touching the door, we must go on to the next level!

In a FOREVER loop, check that IF the key is TOUCHING THE DOOR when it is released by the mouse (NOT MOUSE DOWN). If this is happening, THEN the key will broadcast the message OPEN DOOR and will HIDE.
Remember to stop this Script right after you make the key hide. This is because we are in a FOREVER block, and if we don't stop it, the key will continue to broadcast the message OPEN DOOR, and everything in the game will continue to act accordingly.

THE OPEN DOOR

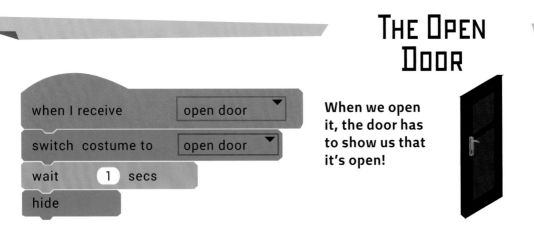

When we open it, the door has to show us that it's open!

When the key receives the message OPEN DOOR, it has to switch to the costume OPEN DOOR.
Then, after 1 second, it can hide, because the first level is complete.

Why does it have to wait 1 second before hiding? Because the computer carries out commands very quickly: if we tell to switch the Sprite's costume and then to hide it immediately after, our eye wouldn't even have time to see the change in costume, but only the Sprite hiding itself.

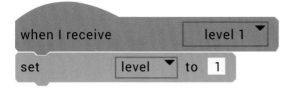

Now's the time when we have to keep track of the levels, because according to how many times the door is opened, we'll be on one level and not another.

Create then the variable LEVEL and set it to 1 when the Stage receives the message LEVEL 1.

Now, every time the door is opened, the level will have to go up by 1. To make this happen, use the block CHANGE LEVEL BY 1 and place it under the Event WHEN I RECEIVE OPEN DOOR.

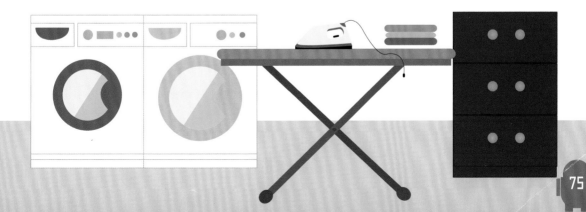

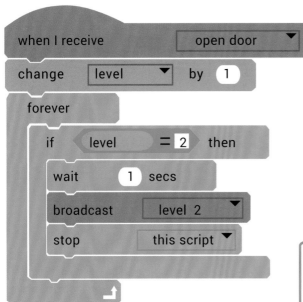

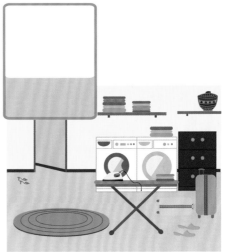

After changing the level, the Stage has to send the right message according to the new level that has to start:
If level 2 is starting, it has to send the message LEVEL 2.

In a FOREVER loop, check that IF the LEVEL is EQUAL TO 2, THEN after 1 second (needed for the door to switch its costume from closed to open) BROADCAST the new message "Level 2." Then STOP THIS SCRIPT.

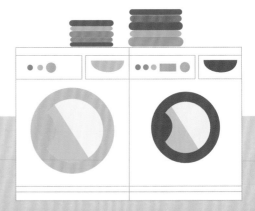

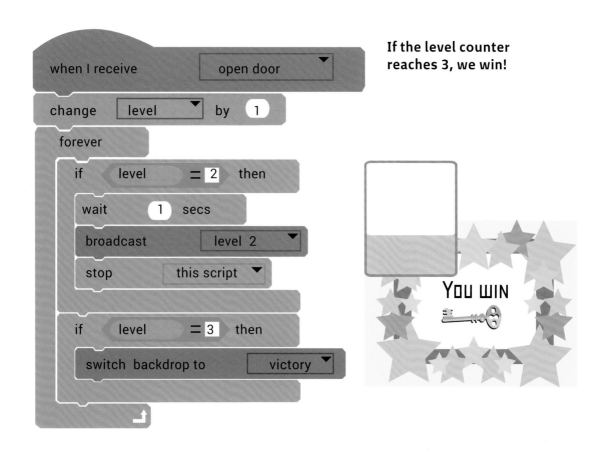

If the level counter reaches 3, we win!

```
when I receive        open door ▼

change  level ▼  by  1

forever
    if  level  = 2  then
        wait  1  secs
        broadcast  level 2 ▼
        stop  this script ▼

    if  level  = 3  then
        switch backdrop to  victory ▼
```

YOU WIN

In the same FOREVER loop, check whether the level counter is at 3; if it is, the SWITCH BACKDROP TO WIN.

HOLD ON!
WE HAVEN'T
WON YET!
LET'S KEEP
PROGRAMMING!

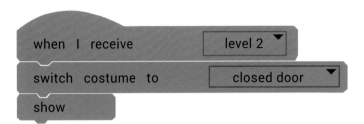

When the second level starts, the door that was opened and hidden, has to close and appear!

```
when I receive          level 2 ▼
switch costume to        closed door ▼
show
```

If you want to put the door in another place in the second room, between the blocks SWITCH COSTUME TO and SHOW, place a block GO TO X:, Y: with the new coordinates of the door.

SECOND LEVEL: THE KEY

```
when I receive          level 2 ▼
go to   x: 160  y: -101
show
```

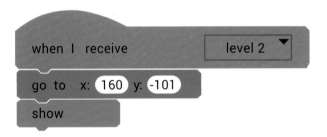

The key, when it receives the level 2 message, will also have to go to its position and appear.

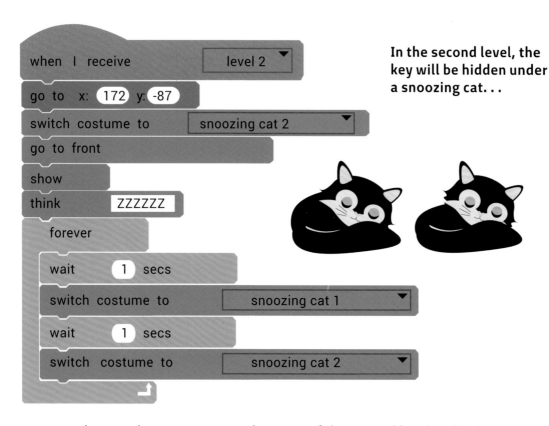

In the second level, the key will be hidden under a snoozing cat. . .

Position the cat where you want in the room of the second level and lock its position by inserting the command GO TO X:, Y: under the event WHEN I RECEIVE LEVEL 2. Then set the first costume the cat will have: which in this case is the second one.

Take the block GO TO FRONT, because the cat, like the rug before, will need to cover the Sprite of the key. Then add the block SHOW.

To make it clearer that the cat is asleep, add the block THINK ZZZ. Then, make the animation of the cat breathing while it sleeps: make it so that the cat switches FOREVER from one costume to another after 1 second.

Second Level: Wake up the Cat!

To get the key, we'll have to wake the cat up by making noise! We'll do it by using our computer's microphone.

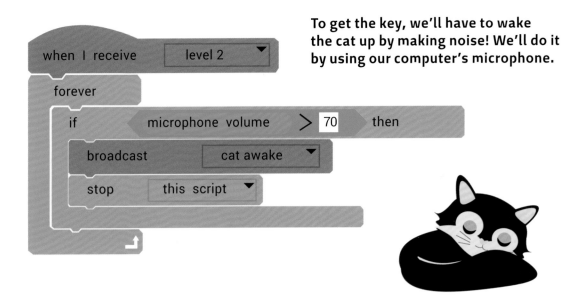

```
when I receive    level 2  ▼
forever
    if        microphone volume  > 70  then
        broadcast       cat awake  ▼
        stop       this script  ▼
```

Scratch lets use the microphone as well: from when it receives the message LEVEL 2, the cat will need to check – FOREVER – whether the volume of the microphone exceeds a certain threshold (70 in this case, but you can change it if you want). IF that happens, THEN it will broadcast the message CAT AWAKE and stop the script.

SECOND LEVEL: THE CAT WAKES UP!

As soon as it wakes up, the cat has to go away so we can get the key.

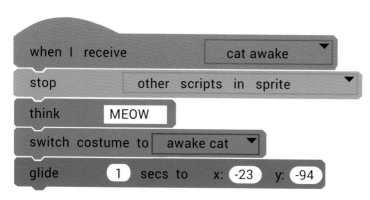

when I receive	cat awake ▼
stop	other scripts in sprite ▼
think	MEOW
switch costume to	awake cat ▼
glide	1 secs to x: -23 y: -94

The first thing that the Sprite has to do when it receives the message CAT AWAKE is to stop all its other scripts. This way the animation of the sleeping cat will stop.

Now the cat can think "Meow" and switch to the CAT AWAKE costume, and then glide to a new position, revealing the key.

INVADERS!

There are two Sprites that have to appear in one level but not in another. How?

VICTORY!

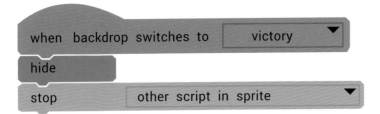

All the Sprites have to hide when we win!

Give this Script to all your Sprites: they all, WHEN THE BACKDROP SWITCHES TO WIN, have to hide and STOP OTHER SCRIPTS IN SPRITE.

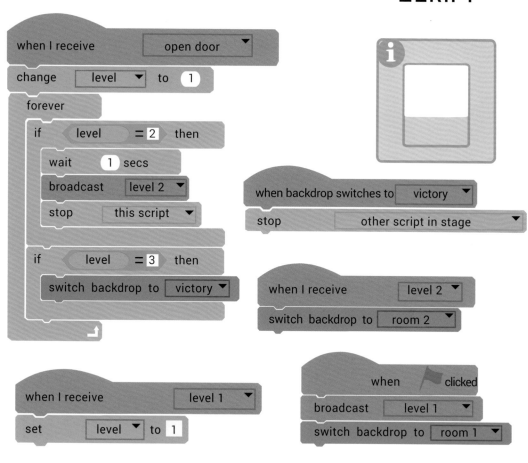

```
when I receive      open door
change  level ▼  to  1
forever
    if  level  = 2  then
        wait  1  secs
        broadcast  level 2 ▼
        stop  this script ▼

    if  level  = 3  then
        switch backdrop to  victory ▼
```

```
when backdrop switches to  victory ▼
stop  other script in stage ▼
```

```
when I receive  level 2 ▼
switch backdrop to  room 2 ▼
```

```
when I receive  level 1 ▼
set  level ▼  to 1
```

```
when ⚑ clicked
broadcast  level 1 ▼
switch backdrop to  room 1 ▼
```

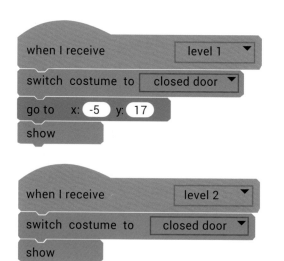

```
when I receive  level 1 ▼
switch costume to  closed door ▼
go to  x: -5  y: 17
show
```

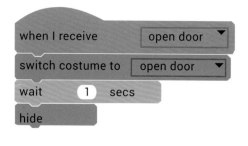

```
when I receive  level 2 ▼
switch costume to  closed door ▼
show
```

```
when I receive  open door ▼
switch costume to  open door ▼
wait  1  secs
hide
```

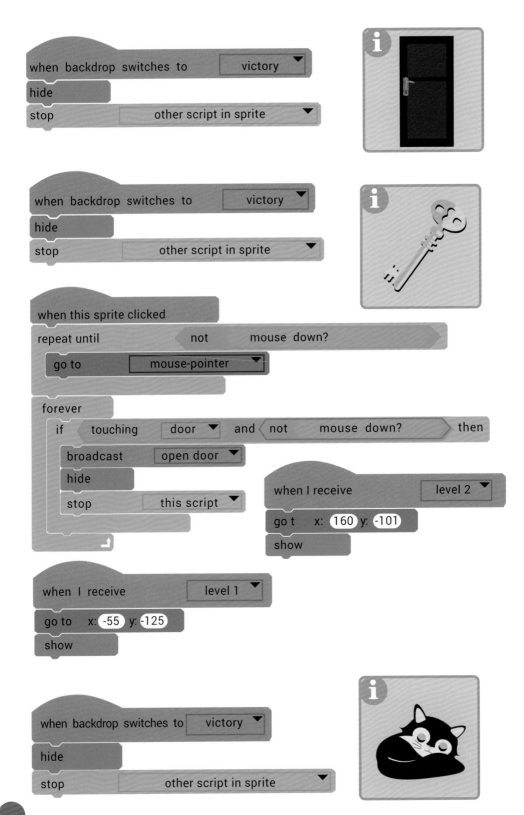

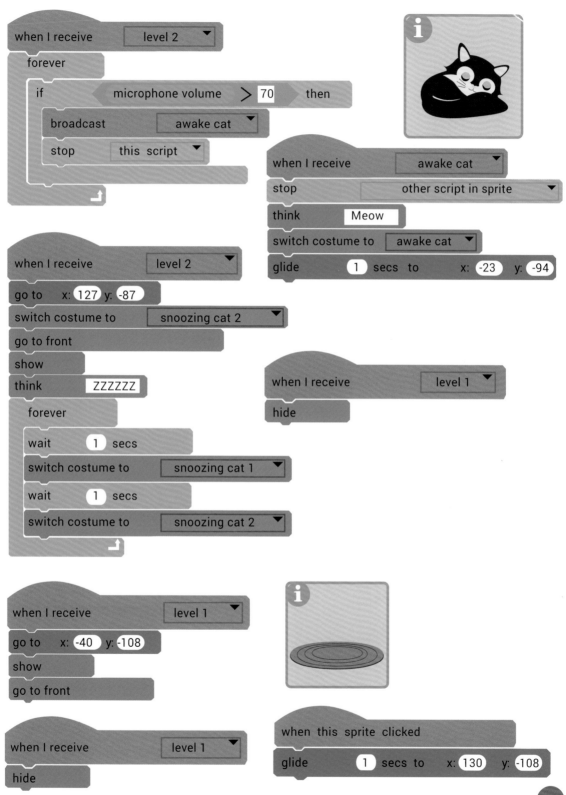

when I receive `level 2`
forever
  if `microphone volume` > `70` then
    broadcast `awake cat`
    stop `this script`

when I receive `awake cat`
stop `other script in sprite`
think `Meow`
switch costume to `awake cat`
glide `1` secs to x: `-23` y: `-94`

when I receive `level 2`
go to x: `127` y: `-87`
switch costume to `snoozing cat 2`
go to front
show
think `ZZZZZZ`
forever
  wait `1` secs
  switch costume to `snoozing cat 1`
  wait `1` secs
  switch costume to `snoozing cat 2`

when I receive `level 1`
hide

when I receive `level 1`
go to x: `-40` y: `-108`
show
go to front

when I receive `level 1`
hide

when this sprite clicked
glide `1` secs to x: `130` y: `-108`

85

CHALLENGE

ADD
AN INTRODUCTION

**Make it so the game doesn't start
immediately with the first level,
but with an introduction screen.**

Try to create a backdrop with the title
of your game, or its rules!

A hint:

Watch out! When the backdrop
is onscreen no Sprites
must be there!

5.

LEVEL

THE SIBYL

5.

THE SIBYL

In the ancient world sibyls were priestesses who were believed to have the power to reveal the future to anyone who paid them a visit.
One of them is ready to reveal your future or someone else's. More or less...

LEVEL:

THE GAME

Decide whether you want to receive a prophecy about your future or about someone else's future.

The Sibyl will cast the leaves, and, mixing up parts of phrases created by you, will read the answer.

A FRIEND'S FUTURE

MY FUTURE

Sprites

Materials

A FRIEND'S FUTURE

MY FUTURE

Backdrops

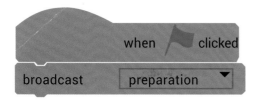

when I clicked

broadcast   preparation ▼

This game will start with a preparation phase: in a few moments, the program will prepare a series of phrases, with which the Sibyl will be able to compose her prophecy.

when I receive   preparation ▼

set   my future ▼   to   false

prepare phrases for my future

prepare phrase for someone else's future

broadcast   preparation end ▼

Create the event "preparation" by using a message, which will be broadcast as soon as the green flag is clicked.

Then create a variable called MY FUTURE and make it so that, at the beginning of the preparation, it is set to "false." You'll make it come true later, if you ask the Sibyl information about your future.

Now click on the category More Blocks. Click on "create a block" and call it "prepare phrases for my future." Then create a second, calling it "prepare phrases for someone else's future."

At this point, put it in the script and BROADCAST the message END PREPARATION.

MORE BLOCKS

The category More Blocks is initially empty, but it allows you to create your own custom blocks.

Click on CREATE A BLOCK, give your new block a name and click on OK.

At this point Scratch will need to know the meaning of the block you have created: it will therefore create a hat block to let you DEFINE the new block. By placing the block under it, you'll be able to decide on the effects of the new command you have created.

But be careful: the blocks you create are only available for the Sprite they have been created for. You can't use them on other Sprites, unless you set up the blocks for them too.

Why create new blocks?

You might want a Sprite to perform a sequence of actions multiple times, for example to appear, glide to a point and disappear. Instead of describing the sequence block by block every time, you can give it a name and reuse it whenever you want, using the new command.

Now let's define the blocks that we have just created. The Sibyl will compose her prophesies by joining a "what" with a "how," for example:
what = you'll tie your shoes
how = jumping on one foot

To better understand what we're doing, imagine that the prophetess picks the "whats" from one cup and the "hows" from another: these two cups will be our two lists.

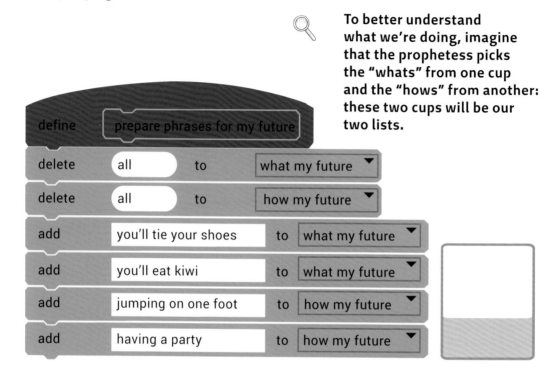

Click on Data and create two lists. One will contain the "whats" for your future and the other will contain the "hows."
To remove it from the screen, remove the mark next to the name of the list, like you've done with other variables before.
First make sure that the lists of "whats" and "hows" are empty at the start of every game. To do this, use the block DELETE ALL OF, for both the lists.
Next, add the phrases you want to put in each of the lists. Remember to put a space at the beginning and at the end of the text.

LISTS

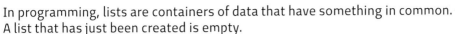

In programming, lists are containers of data that have something in common.
A list that has just been created is empty.
You can add or remove elements to and from a list whenever you want,
and do things to all the elements or just some of them.
In Scratch you can create lists of letters, words, phrases, or numbers.

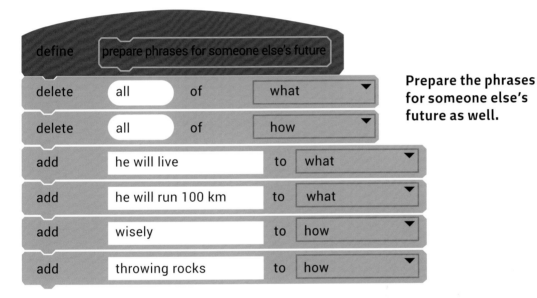

Prepare the phrases for someone else's future as well.

Create two more lists, one for the "whats" and one for the "hows."
Once again choose the phrases you want and how many you want.
The more you add, the more varied the prophecies will be.
Just remember that for your future the Sibyl will be talking directly to the player
(for example, "you'll live"), but this time you'll need to use the third person
(for example, "he or she will live") because she'll be talking about someone else!

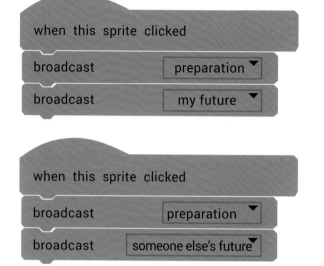

When she is consulted, the Sibyl will want to know whether the prophecy is for the player or for someone else.

Both the buttons, if clicked, will broadcast the PREPARATION message to everyone, so that the prophecy can be created.

But first, they will send a different message, which will let the Sibyl know whether the prophecy is about the player or about someone else. This way, every time you click on one of the two buttons the game will start over.

The Sibyl

Make it so that the Sibyl appears only when the preparation is complete.

When the Sprite of the Sibyl receives the message PREPARATION, she'll need to HIDE. And as soon as she received the end of preparation message, she can go to the front and SHOW herself.

Your Future

When the Sibyl receives the message MY FUTURE, after 1 second she will ask the name of the person whose future you want to know about!

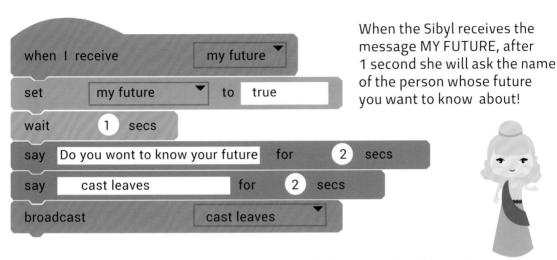

Then she will tell us that she's going to cast the leaves and will broadcast the message CAST LEAVES.

A Friend's Future

To reveal someone else's future, the Sibyl will need to know his or her name.

When the Sibyl receives the message SOMEONE ELSE'S FUTURE, after 1 second she will ask the name of the person whose future you want to know about.
She will save the answer in a "name" variable, exactly like you did with the dragon in the third project.
Then she will tell us that she's going to cast the leaves and will broadcast the message CAST LEAVES.

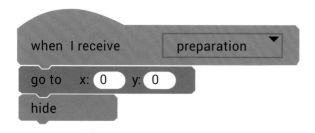

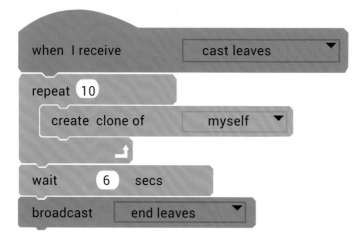

At this point, everything is ready for the leaves to be cast. Some sibyls actually did use to write their prophecies on leaves, which would then be mixed up by the wind.

During the preparation, the leaf Sprite will stay hidden, at the center of the Stage (x: 0, y: 0), behind the Sibyl who'll be in front of it.

As soon as it receives the message CAST LEAVES, it will create 10 clones of itself. Six seconds later, it will broadcast the message END LEAVES, to communicate that the casting is complete.

THE FLIGHT OF THE LEAVES

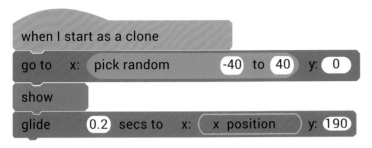

Let's create a realistic movement for the leaves thrown up into the air. What's the first thing an object does when it is thrown upwards? Weee, it goes up of course!

To make it so that the leaves don't just rise in a single file, the newly cloned leaf will first have to move slightly to the right or to the left from where it starts. So let's order it to go to a position with GO TO X PICK RANDOM -40 TO 40, and then to appear.

Every clone will then glide for an instant upwards. Use the number 190 as the Y coordinate, the X has to remain the one that has just been chosen randomly: use the block "X position."

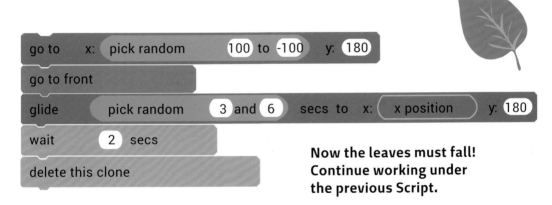

Now the leaves must fall! Continue working under the previous Script.

Now that they're up high, the leaves shouldn't all fall in the same place! Make it so that before falling from up high, at Y: 180, they move a bit to the right and to the left, reaching a RANDOM NUMBER FROM -100 to 100.

Now they will go to the front so that they fall in front of the Sibyl, and then they will glide for a random number of seconds to the ground (Y -180), maintaining their X POSITION.

After 2 seconds the clone will be deleted: this is so we don't find it in the next casting screen.

And now for the Prophecy!

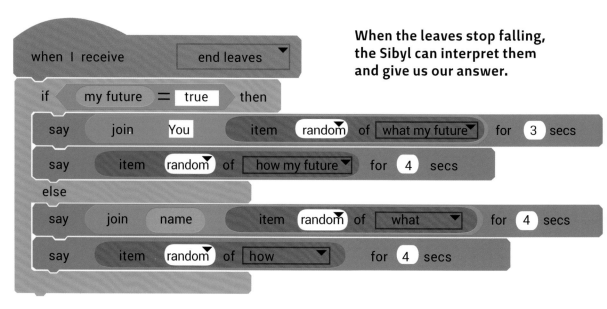

When the leaves stop falling, the Sibyl can interpret them and give us our answer.

when I receive `end leaves`

if `my future` = `true` then

  say join `You` (item `random` of `what my future`) for `3` secs

  say (item `random` of `how my future`) for `4` secs

else

  say join `name` (item `random` of `what`) for `4` secs

  say (item `random` of `how`) for `4` secs

When the Sibyl Sprite receives the message END LEAVES, she will check by means of the variables whether you've asked her to give a prophecy about your future or about someone else's. Therefore, IF the variable MY FUTURE is equal to "true," THEN the Sibyl will say a phrase made up of a "You" and a random element from the "what" list, and then a random element from the "how" list, always about the player's future.

Or ELSE, i.e. if we have asked about someone else's future, she'll say: NAME and a random element from the "what" list, then a random element from the "how" list.

I DON'T THINK YOU NEED
THE COMPLETE SCRIPT ANYMORE!

I'M SURE YOU'RE ALREADY DONE AND
ARE BUSY QUESTIONING THE SIBYL!

BY THE WAY. . . ASK HER SOMETHING
ABOUT MY FUTURE!

CHALLENGE

WHERE?

Make everything even more fun!

For now the Sibyl only says what and how something will happen, but she doesn't say where. Create a new category of phrase to use in making her prophecies!

A hint:

Use lists!

6.

LEVEL

THE SNAIL
RACETRACK

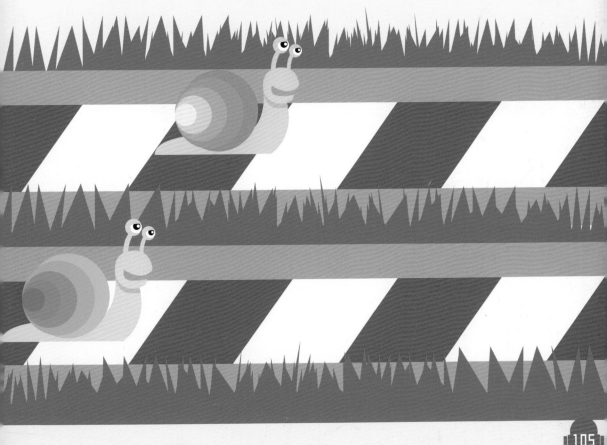

6.

THE SNAIL RACETRACK

Two snails are racing at wild speeds to get to a leaf of lettuce. Who will get there first?

LEVEL:

THE GAME

Challenge a friend!

Wait your turn, draw a card. . . and cross your fingers!

WHAT YOU'LL LEARN:

- To create a game with turns for multiple players

- To create a dice system that affects the game

SPRITES

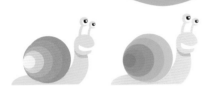

MATERIALS

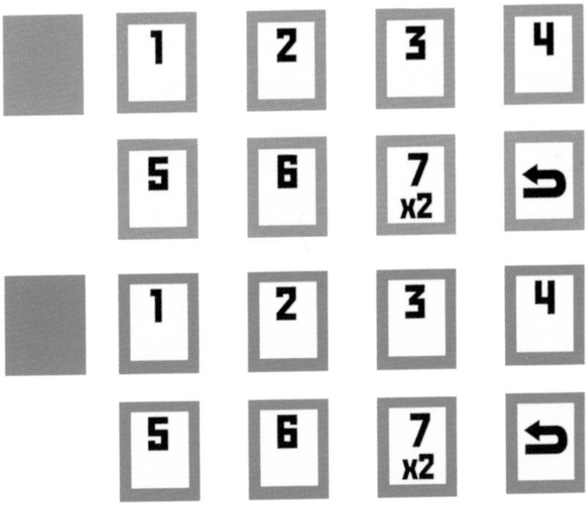

1	2	3	4

| 5 | 6 | 7 x2 | � |

1	2	3	4

| 5 | 6 | 7 x2 | ↩ |

BACKDROPS

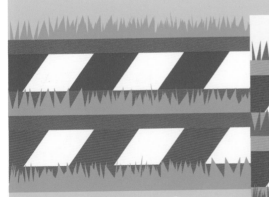

The main elements of this game will be two snails and two decks of cards.

We'll look only at the Scripts for the first player and the first deck. The Scripts for the second player and the second deck will be nearly identical, the only things you'll have to change are the names of the variables and the messages.

When we're done, you'll just have to duplicate all the Scripts for the first snail and first deck and drag them into the second snail and second deck, respectively. Keep in mind that every time a message or a variable contains "player 1," that message or variable will need to be replaced with one for "player 2."

THESE ARE THE VARIABLES YOU'LL NEED:

player 1 Turn

player 2 Turn

C G 1   which stands for "Card drawn by player 1"

C G 2   which stands for "Card drawn by player 2"

AND THESE ARE THE MESSAGES:

player 1 moves ▼

player 2 moves ▼

player 1 double turn ▼

player 2 double turn ▼

player 1 back to the start ▼

player 2 back to the start ▼

player 1 wins ▼

player 2 wins ▼

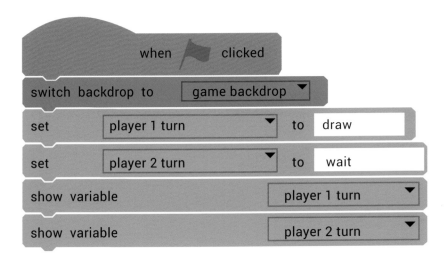

As mentioned, this a game where players take turns: players must be able to draw a card only when it's their turn!

First create two variables: "player 1 turn" and "player 2 turn." On the game screen, place them next to the deck of the player they belong to.

In the Stage, make it so that at the start of the game the backdrop is the right one, and then set the first player's turn to "draw" and the second player's to "wait."

Finally, make the two variables appear.

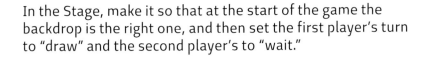

THE DECK OF CARDS

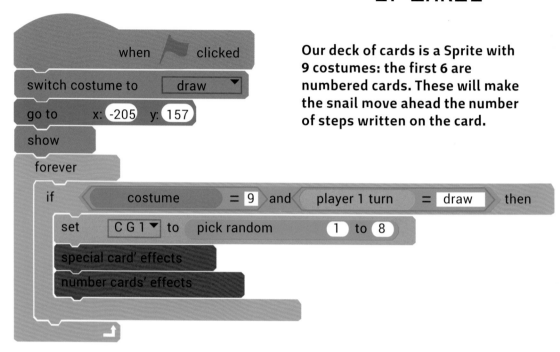

Our deck of cards is a Sprite with 9 costumes: the first 6 are numbered cards. These will make the snail move ahead the number of steps written on the card.

Costumes number 7 and 8 instead are special cards, whose effects we will deal with later on.

Finally, there's the "draw" costume, number 9, which is the one that depicts the back of the card. In order to be able to draw a card, the following conditions must be present:

1. The deck must have the "draw" costume.
2. It must be our turn.

At the start of the game the deck must be wearing the "draw" costume. Then it has to go to the right spot of the Stage and appear. Now, FOREVER, it will check whether the two conditions that are needed to draw are present. When the conditions are true, it will set the variable "C G 1" (player 1's card) to a random number from 1 to 8, then it will check whether you've drawn a number card or a special card. The purple blocks in the image don't exist yet, we'll create them in a moment using the More Blocks function.

110

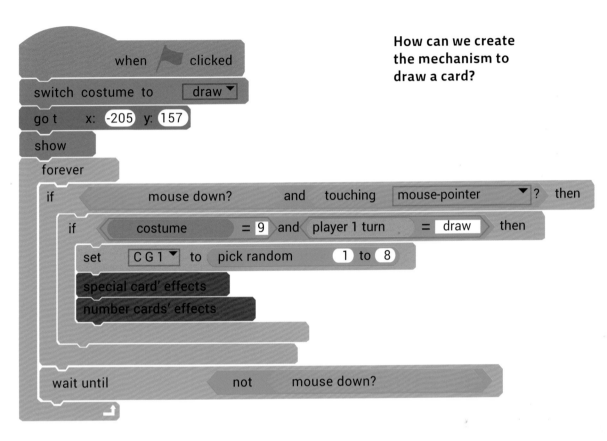

How can we create the mechanism to draw a card?

```
when [flag] clicked
switch costume to [draw ▼]
go t   x: (-205)  y: (157)
show
forever
  if < mouse down?  and  touching [mouse-pointer ▼]? > then
    if < costume = 9 > and < player 1 turn = draw > then
      set [C G 1 ▼] to (pick random (1) to (8))
      special card' effects
      number cards' effects
  wait until < not < mouse down? > >
```

In order to draw a card the player must click on the deck. Now, watch closely, because the next step is a bit complicated: insert the IF. . . THEN you've just created into another IF. . . THEN. This way, the inner command will be activated only if the external command is also active. The game, therefore, will draw a card only IF we are clicking on the deck, that is, if the deck is TOUCHING the cursor of the mouse and if the mouse is clicked.

After this new IF. . . THEN, add the block WAIT UNTIL, and insert a NOT operator followed by MOUSE DOWN.

You've already constructed a Script like this in Game 4, remember?

Number Cards

What happened when you draw a number card?

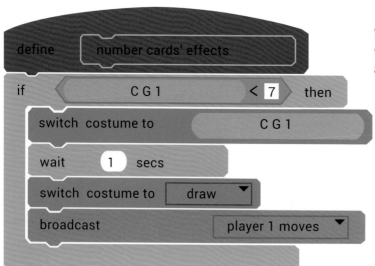

 (8)

Let's look in detail at the new blocks we mentioned before.
We can define them like this:
if the variable C G 1 is less than 7, the card drawn will be a number: so the deck will always have to switch to the costume of the number equal to that of the C G 1 variable. For example, if we draw card number 5, the deck will have to switch to costume number 5.
After waiting 1 second, the deck will go back to its initial costume, and will broadcast the message "player 1 moves."

What if we draw a special card?

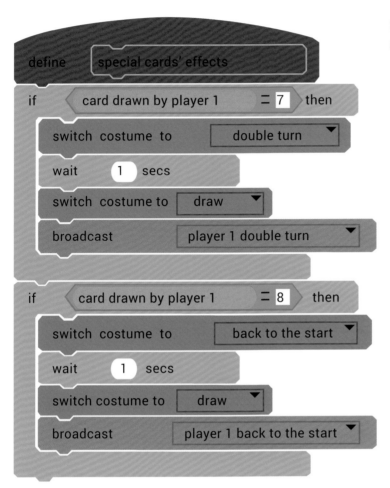

```
define    special cards' effects

if    card drawn by player 1    = 7    then

    switch costume to    double turn ▼

    wait    1    secs

    switch costume to    draw ▼

    broadcast    player 1 double turn ▼


if    card drawn by player 1    = 8    then

    switch costume to    back to the start ▼

    wait    1    secs

    switch costume to    draw ▼

    broadcast    player 1 back to the start ▼
```

If you are lucky enough to draw the seventh card, the deck will switch to the costume "double turn."
One second later, the "draw" costume will return and will broadcast the message "player 1 double turn."
If on the other hand you draw the eighth card, the deck will switch to the costume "back to the start," and after waiting 1 second and returning to its initial costume, the deck will broadcast the message "player 1 back to the start."
You won't have any trouble imagining its effect!

         (8)

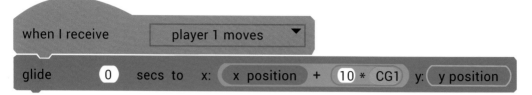

when I receive	player 1 moves ▼

| glide | 0 secs to | x: | x position + 10 * CG1 | y: | y position |

Every time a player draws a number card, the snail will have to move forward. Obviously, the higher the number of the card, the further the snail will go.

To advance, the snail will have to keep its Y POSITION unvaried, and add to its X POSITION the number of the card that's been drawn (C G 1).
But if you add the exact number of the card, the snail will only take tiny steps! Therefore make it so that the number of the card drawn is multiplied by 10 and added to the X position.

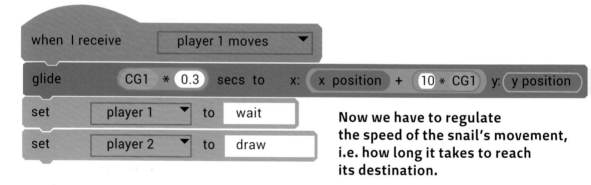

when I receive	player 1 moves ▼

| glide | CG1 * 0.3 secs to | x: | x position + 10 * CG1 | y: | y position |

set	player 1 ▼ to	wait

| set | player 2 ▼ to | draw |

Now we have to regulate the speed of the snail's movement, i.e. how long it takes to reach its destination.

Make the snail glide in C G 1 * 0.3 seconds. This way our hero will move slowly for short distances, and more quickly for longer distances.
Let's make some examples:
If the card drawn is 1, the snail will need to go a short way, and as 1 x 0.3 = 0.3, it will glide for 0.3 seconds.
If the card drawn is 6, the snail will go a longer way. So it will take a bit longer, and indeed 6 x 0.3 = 1.8 seconds.

Once the snail has completed its movement, it will be the next player's turn.
So the snail that has just moved will set its turn to "wait," and the other player's snail will set its turn to "draw."

DOUBLE TURN

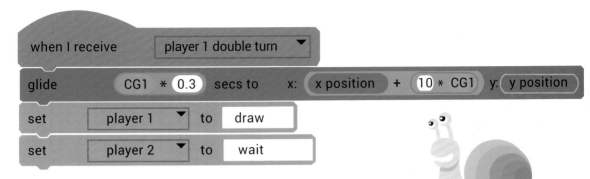

```
when I receive    player 1 double turn ▼

glide    CG1 * 0.3 secs to   x: ( x position + 10 * CG1 )  y: ( y position )

set    player 1 ▼   to   draw

set    player 2 ▼   to   wait
```

When a player draws the "double turn" card, the snail Sprite will advance exactly like before. The only difference is that this time it won't give up its turn, but will have another move. So "player 1 turn" will remain set to "draw" and "player 2 turn" to "wait."

BACK TO THE START

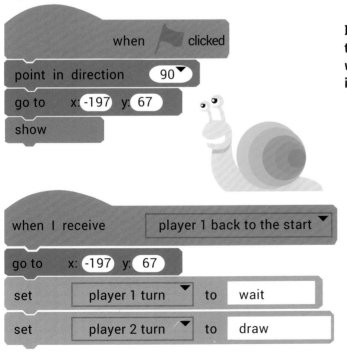

```
when 🏳 clicked

point in direction  90 ▼

go to    x: -197  y: 67

show
```

```
when I receive    player 1 back to the start ▼

go to    x: -197  y: 67

set    player 1 turn ▼   to   wait

set    player 2 turn ▼   to   draw
```

If you draw the card "back to the start," the snail will have to go back to its starting position.

First of all, at the beginning of the game the snail will have to be facing to the right, go to its position and appear.

Then when the player draws the card "back to the start," the snail will have to reposition itself at the same coordinates it started from and change turns.

LETTUCE!

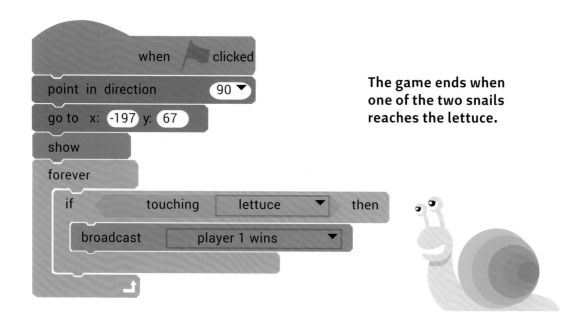

The game ends when one of the two snails reaches the lettuce.

Make it so that the game checks FOREVER whether the snail is TOUCHING the Sprite of the lettuce. If that happens, it will broadcast the message "player 1 wins."
Remember of course to do the same for the other player!

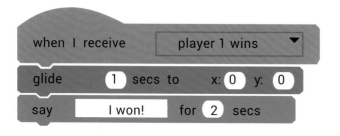

Having reached the finish line, the winning snail should glide to the center of the stage and say "I won" for 2 seconds.
On the other hand, if the other player wins the defeated snail should simply hide.

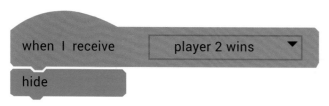

Victory

As soon as the Stage receives one of the two win messages, it will change the backdrop and hide the two turn variables. Then it will stop all its Scripts.

Lettuce!!!

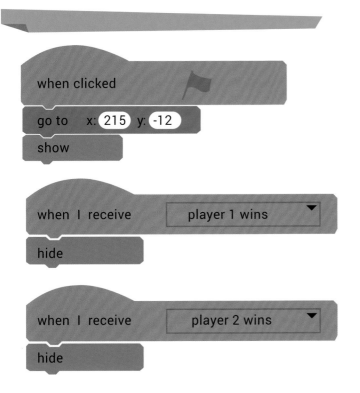

At the beginning of the game the lettuce will take its starting position and appear. At this point it just has to wait for one of the two players to win, to then disappear.

REMEMBER TO GIVE THE COMMANDS TO THE SECOND SNAIL AND THE SECOND DECK TOO, AS YOU READ ON PAGE 108!

CHALLENGE

WHO DRAWS FIRST?

As things currently are in the game, player 1 always goes first.

You can make it so the game chooses randomly who draws first.

A hint:

Come on,
you're an expert now!

SOLUTIONS

120

BUBBLES

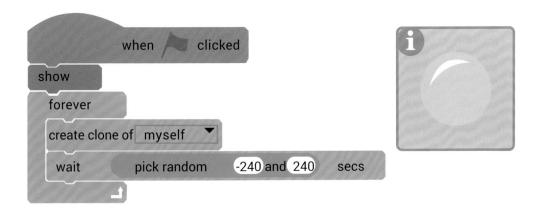

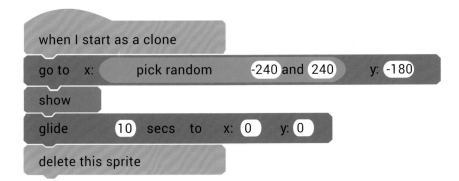

Add the bubble Sprite.
Like you did with the fish, make it so this Sprite hides, and that it's only its clones that appear. This time use a FOREVER loop, so the bubbles keep going until the program is stopped!
As soon as the clone is created make it so that it positions itself at the bottom of the screen (Y: -180) at a random point between the far left (X: -240) and right (X: 240) of the Stage and that it shows itself. Then make it glide in 10 seconds to the center of the Stage (X: 0, Y: 0) to then be deleted.

WHAT WAS THE CORRECT ANSWER?

Under the block SAY "Try again!" put another SAY.
Inside the blank space of this second block, insert a JOIN block.
Now write in the first part "The correct answer was" and in the second put the operation "first number X second number," like you did before to check whether the answer was correct.

if (answer = (first number ✱ second number)) then

    change [right answers ▼] of (1)

    say [Right!] for (2) secs

else

    say [Try again!] for (2) secs

    say (joint (The right answer was) and (first number ✱ second number)) for (2) secs

ADD AN INTRODUCTION

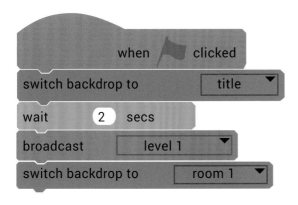

Create your backdrop - remember how? IF not go to page 10 of the introduction.

In the Stage, before sending the message LEVEL 1, make it so that the backdrop switches to the title for 2 seconds.

Then make all the Sprites hide when the green flag is clicked.
The right ones will appear as soon as the LEVEL 1 message is broadcast.

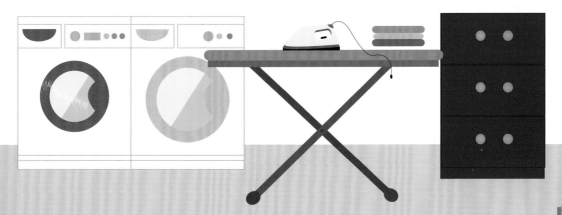

WHERE?

Create a "where" list and make it so it is filled in the Stage, during the preparation. Then, in the Sibyl Sprite, add to the prophecy the block SAY ITEM RANDOM OF WHERE.

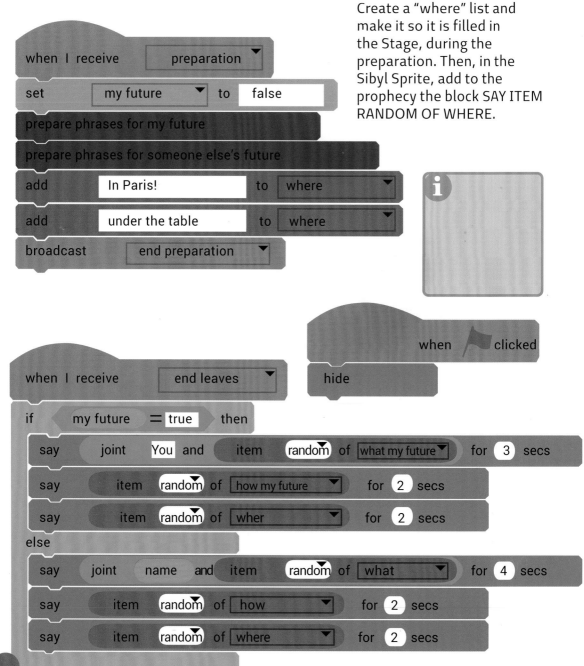

```
when I receive    preparation ▼

set    my future ▼    to    false

prepare phrases for my future

prepare phrases for someone else's future

add    In Paris!    to    where ▼

add    under the table    to    where ▼

broadcast    end preparation ▼
```

```
when 🏳 clicked

hide
```

```
when I receive    end leaves ▼

if    my future = true    then

    say    joint  You  and    item  random▼ of  what my future ▼   for  3  secs

    say    item  random▼ of  how my future ▼   for  2  secs

    say    item  random▼ of  wher ▼   for  2  secs

else

    say    joint  name  and  item  random▼ of  what ▼   for  4  secs

    say    item  random▼ of  how ▼   for  2  secs

    say    item  random▼ of  where ▼   for  2  secs
```

WHO DRAWS FIRST?

```
when 🏳 clicked

show variable        player 1 turn  ▼

show variable        player 2 turn  ▼

switch backdrop to  [backdrop game ▼]

set [ draws first  ▼ ] to ( pick random (1) and (2) )

if < draws first = 1 > then

    set [ player 1 turn  ▼ ] to  draw

    set [ player 2 turn  ▼ ] to  wait

else

    set [ player 1 turn  ▼ ] to  draw

    set [ player 2 turn  ▼ ] to  wait
```

Create the variable "Draws first" and set it to a random number
between 1 and 2 at the start of the game. Then check whether
the 1 has been chosen, IF yes, THEN set "player 1 turn" to "draw"
and "player 2 turn" to "wait," or ELSE do the contrary.

WHAT WE'VE LEARNED:

- To set up a new project
- To create a simple animation
- To create effects with graphics

- To clone Sprites
- To use randomness

- To program a game with questions and answers
- To use variables

- To use messages
- To create a game with levels
- New ways of interacting with Sprites: clicking, using the microphone, drag and drop

- To use lists
- To create onscreen buttons
- To create more blocks

- To create a multi-player game with turns
- To create a dice system that affects the game

DID YOU HAVE FUN? DO YOU WANT TO GO ON? KEEP EXPERIMENTING WITH WHAT YOU HAVE LEARNED BY CREATING NEW GAMES.

REMEMBER THAT SCRATCH IS ALSO A COMMUNITY! ON THE WEBSITE YOU CAN FIND NEW PROJECTS AND SHARE THE ONES YOU MAKE.

IF YOU WANT TO TEST YOURSELF WITH RIDDLES AND ANIMATED STORIES, LOOK FOR OUR FIRST BOOK:

CODING FOR KIDS.
CREATE YOUR OWN VIDEOGAMES WITH SCRATCH

These projects are the result of the experience with the courses and workshops that Coder Kids (www.coderkids. it) has organized and held in schools both as an addition to the teaching curriculum and as an extracurricular activity.

We take the opportunity to thank the children, their families, and their teachers, for having participated with such great enthusiasm and for being a continuous source of inspiration to us.

CODER KIDS

Coder Kids (www.coderkids.it) has been organizing courses of computer programming and robotics for children and teens since 2014. The courses are done both in schools, as an addition to the teaching curriculum, and as an extracurricular activity.

The projects in this book, designed and created by Viviana Figus, Federico Vagliasindi, Federica Gambel and Johan Aludden, are the products of these laboratories.

For White Star Kids Coder Kids also published "Coding for kids. Create your own Videogames with Scratch".

ILLUSTRATIONS
AND GRAPHIC DESIGN BY:

VALENTINA FIGUS

WHITE STAR KIDS

White Star Kids® is a registered trademark property of White Star s.r.l.

© 2017 White Star s.r.l.
Piazzale Luigi Cadorna, 6 - 20123 Milan, Italy
www.whitestar.it

Translation and editing: Iceigeo, Milan (Joshua Burkholder)

ISBN 978-88-544-1218-7
1 2 3 4 5 6   21 20 19 18 17

Printed in Italy by Rotolito Lombarda
Seggiano di Pioltello (MI)